A Stepping-Stone Book

CLOTHES
TELL A STORY
From Skin to Space Suits
By
CECIL and WINIFRED LUBELL

Parents' Magazine Press • New York

Contents

1. Your Favorite Clothes

You get up in the morning and in two minutes you can be dressed for the day.

Two minutes flat! Right? Underpants, socks, shirt, jeans, maybe a belt, sneakers. And most days it's the same for boys and girls.

Those are probably your favorite clothes. They're comfortable. You don't need to worry about spoiling them, or getting them dirty. They're strong. You can play in them.

But suppose you had lived 150 years ago. It was quite different then. This is what a girl had to put on in the morning:

1. First, a long, frilly undershirt.

2. Over that, a tight thing called a bodice, with a lot of buttons in the back.

3. A garter belt to hold up stockings.

4. Long stockings of cotton or wool.

5. Long underpants that were buttoned to the bodice.

6. High buttoned shoes. More buttons!

7. A red flannel petticoat.

8. Another petticoat, this one starched.

9. Over all that, a long stiff dress.

10. Over the dress an apron, called a pinafore, to keep the dress clean.

11. A hair ribbon, tied in a bow.

12. A bonnet, tied under the chin.

That's twelve pieces of clothing. It must have taken those poor girls at least half an hour to get dressed, and someone had to help them fasten all those buttons in the back. There were no zippers in those days.

What about the boys? Almost as bad! This is what a boy had to wear:

1. An undershirt of wool or cotton.
2. Long underpants of wool.
3. A shirt, often with ruffles, and a tie.
4. Long black stockings held up by garters.
5. High buttoned boots.
6. Pants that buttoned onto the shirt.
7. A buttoned-up waistcoat.
8. A wool jacket.
9. A hat and coat.

It would take much more than two minutes to put all that on!

There's another thing that was quite different
in those days. Today, when we need new clothes,
most of us go to a store to buy them. But 150
years ago clothes couldn't be bought in a store.
A tailor or a seamstress had to make them. Or
women made them at home, and all by hand.
There were no sewing machines in those days.

For many people, especially country people,
it was very expensive to get new cloth. In the
families of farmers and other working people
children's clothes were often made from outgrown
clothes of older brothers and sisters, or even
from parents' old clothes. And they might be full
of patches to make them last longer.

When they wanted to buy new cloth, people
often had to wait until a peddler came to their
houses. He sold them cloth and ribbons, buttons,
needles, and thread. Peddlers traveled all over
the land by horse and wagon. Sometimes they
came on foot, carrying packs on their backs. But
they didn't come often; perhaps only once a year.

So you can see it was much harder to get new
clothes in those days than it is today. Children
had to take very good care of the few clothes
they owned so they would last a long time.

They didn't have strong denim jeans as you do today. Jeans were not invented until 1849.

The jeans business was started during the Gold Rush days in California by a man named Levi Strauss. He made pants for the gold miners out of blue denim because it was strong and didn't show dirt. To make them even stronger, Levi Strauss put copper rivets on the pockets so they wouldn't tear when the miners stuffed them with gold nuggets. The pants were such a success that the miners began to call them "Levi's Pants" and now we call them "Levi's" for short.

2. Why We Wear Clothes

Cats don't wear clothes. Birds don't wear clothes. Only people wear clothes. Why is that?

One reason is that clothes keep us warm. Cats have furry skins to keep them warm, and birds have feathers. Our clothes take the place of fur and feathers. People in very cold lands —like the Eskimos in Alaska—must have clothes to stay alive.

But most of us don't live in such cold places. What's more, most of us live in heated houses, and we certainly don't need all the clothes we wear indoors in winter.

We don't need clothes to keep us warm in
summer, but we still wear them, even when we
go to the seashore. So there must be other reasons
why we wear clothes.

One other reason is that most people are not
used to going about naked. It wasn't always so.
In earliest times, people in hot climates didn't
know about clothes, and it was natural for them
to be naked. There are still some who live
like that in hot lands.

We also wear clothes so that people will know who we are. You can recognize a policeman by his clothes, or an airplane pilot, or an ice-cream man. And you can tell a boy from a girl by their clothes, though that's not so easy to do nowadays. Even in ancient times, a king and queen could be recognized by their crowns and jewels.

Perhaps the chief reason we wear clothes is simply because we like them. We like the way we look in clothes and we think they make other people like us more. We wear them as decorations. Far back in history people wore clothes for that reason, even when they didn't need them to keep warm.

A king and queen in ancient Egypt

3. The First Clothes

The earliest people we know anything about lived in hot climates where they didn't need clothes and didn't wear any. They decorated their bodies with paint and with ornaments made of shells, and animal teeth, and even fishbones.

Clothes came much later. In the beginning they were not for decoration but for warmth. Some of those early people moved from warm to colder lands. They were not used to the cold and they needed clothing just to keep warm.

They could see that animals with hairy skins didn't mind the cold, so they began to make clothes for themselves out of those skins. With sharp stone knives they cleaned the skins and sewed them together with bone needles. For thread they used animal sinews or horsehair.

Many thousands of years later, people discovered that they didn't need to kill wild animals in order to get clothes. They learned how to clip the hair of wild animals and make cloth with it. Still later, they became farmers instead of hunters. They raised sheep and goats and used their wool to spin and weave cloth.

How did they do this?

The first clothes were made from skins

*Spinning wool
in ancient Greece*

You can find out for yourself, if you use a ball of absorbent cotton instead of wool. Look carefully and you'll see that the ball is a loose bundle of short, thin threads. We call them fibers. Now, if you pull out some of these fibers gently, and roll them between your fingers as you pull, you can make a string.

That's called spinning, and the string is called a yarn.

If you twist the yarn tightly it gets to be quite strong, even though it's made of short fibers. And, if you keep on pulling and twisting, you can gradually make the yarn as long as you like and wind it into a ball.

This is just what early people did. It was the first step in learning to make cloth.

The next step was to take a lot of those yarns and turn them into cloth. People learned to tie them to a stick in long rows and then to cross the rows under and over with other yarns.

That's called weaving.

Wool was not the only fiber those early people used for making cloth. They used fibers from many plants, especially the flax and cotton plants. They also learned how to unwind the silk threads from insect cocoons and weave that into cloth as well.

These four fibers—wool, flax, cotton, and silk—were the chief materials used by all early people for making cloth and clothes. Natural fibers such as these were the only ones used until recent times. We still use them today.

In weaving, threads are crossed over and under each other

4. Clothes Tell a Story

The first clothes made from cloth were very simple clothes and they were just about the same for men and women. In each part of the world they were made from the special materials found in that place. Some countries had wool. Others had flax, or cotton, or silk. In some places the stems of plants such as jute and milkweed were used.

In each country the clothes looked a little
different because they had to suit the climate
and the customs of the people who lived there.
But, in one way, all the clothes of those early
times were alike because they were long and loose.
Many of them were just big pieces of cloth,
like blankets, which people draped over their
bodies in different ways.

These first clothes were not cut and sewn to
fit the body, as most clothes are today. No
sizes were needed. One size could be draped to
fit all men and women—tall and short,
fat and thin.

It was very practical. They didn't need to put their clothes on hangers in closets. They folded them flat and stored them in boxes. They probably didn't need to press them either, but simply washed them and hung them out to dry.

The people of ancient Greece had simple clothes like these. Each garment was one piece of wool or cotton cloth. It was draped over the body in different ways. Sometimes it was pinned at the shoulder and sometimes it was tied at the waist with a belt. It always looked graceful and was comfortable to wear.

The long dresses of Greek women were called *chitons* (kȳ-tons). When it got cold they added another piece of cloth and wore it like a shawl, over the *chiton*. A Greek man had the same kind of *chiton*, draped in a different way, but he often used only a big shawl wrapped around his body. Farmers and other workers had shorter *chitons*, and so did the children.

Clothes of the ancient Greeks were comfortable, simple, and handsome

Clothes like those of ancient Greece are still
worn today in some parts of the world.

In India, women still wear a garment called a
sari (sah-ree), as they did in ancient times. It
is a long piece of beautiful cloth, and they
wrap it around themselves in a very special way.
Sometimes the cloth is woven with golden designs.
It is a very good garment for the hot climate of
India. At the United Nations in New York you
can often see women from India dressed in *saris*.

In Mexico and in South America men and
women wear ponchos, as they have done for
hundreds of years. The poncho is also just one
piece of cloth—like a blanket—but it has a hole in
the middle so that it can be slipped over the head
on top of other clothes. This is a good idea in
these countries where it is often hot during the
day, but cool when the sun goes down. When it
is too warm, people can simply fold up their
ponchos and carry them over their shoulders.
Ponchos are now popular in the United States.

In many countries of Africa people wear
clothes like those of the ancient Greeks. The
people of the desert wear long, loose robes of
cotton or wool, which cover them from head to
foot. These protect them from sun and sandstorms.

In other African countries women wear two
pieces of cloth printed with bright designs. One
is like a skirt; the other like a shawl.

Men in these countries often wear long robes
made with colorful bands of cloth sewn together.
They are called *kente* robes.

For hundreds of years clothes in most parts
of the world looked like the Greek clothes. Then,
about 700 years ago, they began to change. People
learned to cut and sew fabrics the way we do
today. Clothes were made to fit the shape of the
body. Because of this they looked quite different
from Greek clothes. People now wore several
fitted garments, one on top of the other.

The biggest change of all was this: men's and women's clothes began to look different. Men's garments became much shorter. Some of them looked like a girl's mini-dress today. Men also wore long stockings, much like the ones women wear today. They didn't fit as well as modern stockings because they were not knitted.

Women's dresses continued to be very long, with wide skirts, tight waists, and sometimes with sleeves that hung almost to the ground.

Clothes kept on changing through the years. In England, 400 years ago, they were terribly stiff and unnatural. A nobleman and his wife dressed in fancy silks and lace and velvet. Even the children were dressed the same way. They all wore stiff, pleated collars called ruffs.

People certainly didn't expect to do any work in such clothes. In fact, they probably dressed like that to show that they were wealthy and didn't need to work at all.

Working people of those times looked quite different. They wore very simple clothes, often ragged and patched, because they couldn't afford anything better. Usually their clothes were dark blue, like denim jeans today, because that was the cheapest dye color in those days.

This is what a working man and his family looked like at that time:

In America, during Colonial times, clothes
began to change again, but in a different way.
The Puritans who came to the New World from
England were not rich people. They had to work
hard. They couldn't afford fancy clothes. They
wanted their clothes to be neat and simple and
to last a long time.

There was a big difference between the clothes
of Puritans in New England and the clothes of
fashionable people in old England.

However, after 100 years in the New World, Americans grew wealthy and wanted to look like the rich people of the old world. The men began to wear wigs, three-cornered hats, fancy waistcoats, knee breeches, and white silk stockings. George Washington dressed like that.

The ladies wore long silk gowns with frilly sleeves, and small lace caps. They followed the fashions of the times by sending to London and Paris for dolls dressed up like the fashionable ladies in those cities. Then they had the doll clothes copied for themselves.

The pioneers who later went west in America couldn't have worn such clothes. Their clothes had to be working clothes. A pioneer woman in the West couldn't buy clothes, even if she could afford them. There were no stores in the frontier lands. She had to make all the clothes for herself and her family. That meant she had to grow the fiber, spin the yarn, weave the cloth, and then sew it by hand.

So you can see that the pioneer woman and her
daughter wouldn't have looked at all like the
wife and daughter of a rich city merchant. By
that time the American merchant's family looked
like fashionable women in Europe. They were so
dressed up that they could hardly move around in
their tight dresses, two or three stiff petticoats,
and huge skirts.

*Iroquois hunter with
shaved head, called a* roach

What a difference between these clothes and
the clothes of the Indians who lived in America
long before the settlers came.

There were many tribes of Indians in America.
Their clothes were not all the same because they
lived far apart. The climate and the materials
for clothes were different in each place.

Some Indians wore deerskin clothes and big
head-dresses of feathers. Others made cloth of
milkweed, or cotton, or wool. And some used
cedar bark, which they pounded until it was soft.

The Woodland Indians of the Iroquois tribe
were the ones the Puritans met. These Indians
had no cloth. Their clothes were made from soft
deerskin and were often beautifully embroidered
with porcupine quills.

Usually they wore very few clothes. Iroquois men tied two small deerskin aprons around their waists—one in front and one in back. They had deerskin leggings and moccasins. Iroquois women wore deerskin skirts with fringes, and sometimes short deerskin dresses. In cold weather both men and women used fur robes.

Their faces and bodies were painted and they wore necklaces of shells and bones. Iroquois women braided their hair, but the men often shaved their heads except for a narrow strip on top. This was called a roach. It was decorated with turkey feathers.

They had no pockets in their clothes so they carried deerskin pouches around their waists.

Indian clothes lasted a long time and were very practical for a hard way of life. The pioneers knew this, and some of them—like Daniel Boone—began to wear deerskin clothes themselves, as some of us still do today.

Indian deerskin pouch

5. Top to Toe

Clothes make a big difference in the way people look. All through history they have been used to show that difference—between rich and poor, between men and women, between one country and another, between one time and another.

The way people looked at different times in history is called the fashion of the times, and the fashions of long ago are often repeated in the clothes we wear today.

From top to toe—from our hair styles to our shoes—we sometimes look just like the people of bygone times.

6. TOP: Hair and Hats

High hats, low hats, long hair, short hair, fancy hair, plain hair, wigs for men, wigs for women—all this has been going on for thousands of years. It's still going on today.

Very few of these styles were meant to protect the head. Most of them were for decoration. It was the fashion of the times.

Long hair for men and boys is not a new idea. Until modern times most men had long hair. And long ago some people were annoyed by this, just as they are today. The Puritans even had a rule against long hair for men.

George Washington wore a wig and so did most other men in those days. Their wigs were often covered with white powder to make them fancier. The king of France had a much bigger wig. (He really was a bigwig!) And a lady of fashion wore a hairdo so high that she had to sleep sitting up for fear of spoiling it.

Today a few men wear high hats to weddings, but in Abe Lincoln's day men wore them every day. That was the fashion of his time.

7. MIDDLE: Shirts and Jackets

The history of clothes begins with the shirt. The short Greek *chiton* was a kind of shirt. Later, the shirt became longer and was called a shift. It was worn next to the skin by men and women, day and night. They slept in it.

After that it got shorter and fancier. Women called it a blouse. They often decorated it with embroidery and wore it with a laced-up vest.

Men's shirts had ruffles and lace at the collar and cuffs. In your grandfather's time the collars and cuffs were buttoned onto the shirt so they could be taken off and washed without washing the whole shirt.

Long ago people began to wear decorated jackets over their shirts. Some men's jackets were pullovers called tunics. Others were called doublets and were made with lace frills or with cutouts to show the colorful linings.

And there were capes, all kinds of capes. A lady wore a velvet party cape lined with fur. A gentleman wore a coat with several capes, one over the other.

Today people are again beginning to wear clothes very much like these.

8. BOTTOM: Pants and Skirts

People once thought only men should wear pants and women should wear skirts. That's certainly not the way it goes today. What's more, it was not that way in the past either.

The women of Persia and China always wore pants and still do. Some men in Scotland and in Greece always wore skirts and still do. In Colonial times a boy wore skirts until he was five years old, when he got his first breeches.

42

In 1851 an American woman named Amelia
Bloomer started a great fuss by wearing floppy
pants with a skirt. People made fun of her but
Mrs. Bloomer wanted to show that women's skirts
in those days were ridiculous.

And they really were! They were often ten
yards around, like tents, and were held up by
big wire frames. Even little girls wore them.
How did they ever sit down in those skirts?

All of which shows that fashion can get
pretty silly at times.

9. TOE: Shoes

Some of the silliest—and some of the most sensible—things in fashion are shoes.

The most sensible ones are sandals. The ancient Greeks wore them and we wear them today. Moccasins are sensible, too, and we got them from the Indians. So are firemen's boots, which we got from horseback riding boots of earlier times.

There were other shoes in the past that looked silly but were really practical. These were the wooden shoes, or the shoes with high platforms.

In those days there were no paved sidewalks and the streets were thick with mud. The platform shoes kept people above the mud.

The silliest shoes were the ones with high heels or pointed toes, which ruined the feet. They were worn by people who wanted to show they were rich and didn't need to work or ever walk in the mud. Sometimes the toes were so long that people tripped over them.

10. UNDERNEATH: Corsets

Imagine this: a thick vest, without sleeves, that looked like a piece of armor but was made of cloth. It stood up by itself because strips of bone or steel were sewn into the cloth. It was wrapped around the body and laced up tight at the back to squeeze in the waist.

That was a corset and that's what a fashionable lady wore 100 years ago.

Even children wore them. As soon as a little girl was old enough to walk, she was laced into a corset. This was supposed to make her stand up straight, but it certainly wasn't healthy.

11. Work Clothes

There's another reason for wearing clothes besides the reasons mentioned before. Clothes also protect people in their work.

The first work clothing was probably the armor worn by soldiers in ancient times. Another kind was the leather apron and knee pads worn by coal miners long ago. After leather aprons came all kinds of cloth aprons—for cooks, waiters, and many others, including the apron your mother wears when she's working in the kitchen.

In modern times the apron became the overall and the coverall worn by such people as farmers, carpenters, and mechanics. From the coverall came

the diving suit, and the fire-fighting suit of asbestos, and finally the space suit which costs as much as $100,000 for just one man.

And, of course, there are work clothes for such people as baseball and football players.

Work clothes like these all came about within the last 100 years. Before that very few special clothes were made for work, except the denim jeans of Mr. Levi Strauss. Most working clothes were just old clothes. In George Washington's time, working men generally wore heavy linen shirts, thick wool breeches with a belt, wool stockings, and shoes with thick wooden soles. To makes the breeches last longer they were the same at front and back. If the seat wore out, they could be turned back to front.

All through history people had another sort of work clothing, not to protect themselves, but to show the kind of work they did. For example, 300 years ago doctors used to wear long black robes, and so did lawyers. Today, a judge wears the same kind of robe in court, and a minister wears one in church.

In the same way the uniforms worn by policemen, firemen, and soldiers are their work clothes. So are the clothes of a nurse and an airplane stewardess, and a doorman in front of a hotel.

Look around your neighborhood and you'll find many other people wearing clothes which tell you where they work or what kind of work they do.

A simple loom in ancient Egypt

12. Cloth Makes Clothes

What is cloth?

Cloth is a flat material made by putting together yarns or fibers in several ways.

Earlier in this book you found out how people learned to spin yarns and turn them into cloth by weaving. For this they invented the loom.

The first looms were very simple. Yarns were hung from a stick like a curtain rod. To hold them straight, weights were tied to the bottom. Then another yarn was woven from side to side, in and out of the hanging yarns. The hanging yarns were called warp yarns. The in-and-out yarns were called weft yarns.

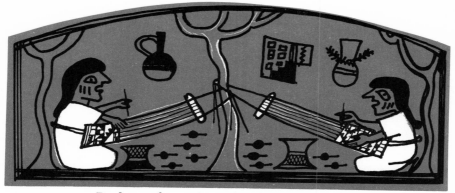

Backstrap looms in ancient painting

Later, the loom was turned sideways so it lay flat. The top stick was tied to a tree. The bottom ends of the warp yarns were attached to another stick, which was tied to the waist of the weaver who could then sit on the ground to weave. This is the way weaving is still done today in some parts of the world. That kind of loom is called a backstrap loom.

Through the centuries people kept improving the loom. They didn't change the method of weaving. They only made it faster. But not as fast as you might think. An old loom could make a yard of fabric in an hour. A modern machine loom is only about twelve times faster.

Even so, weaving is still the most important method used in making cloth today.

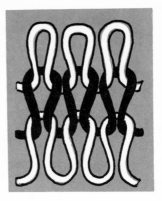

Knitting stitches

The next most important method is knitting. In weaving, two separate sets of yarns cross over each other in opposite directions. In knitting, only one yarn is used and this is crossed over itself to make stitches. People do that when they knit sweaters. First they make one row of stitches. Then they connect a second row to the first, and so on until they have a piece of cloth shaped like a sweater. They could make a long piece of cloth the same way.

Today, these two kinds of cloth are made mostly by electric power machines, but until 150 years ago they were all made by hand or by hand machines. And until about 80 years ago they were

Modern electric knitting machines

made only with natural fibers such as wool, flax, cotton, and silk. But in 1889 a French scientist named Hilaire Chardonnet (shar-donn-ay) invented a way to make fibers from chemicals.

For hundreds of years scientists had been watching silkworms spin their cocoons and they had been trying to imitate the silkworm by making silk-like fibers from chemicals. Many men tried, but no one really succeeded until Chardonnet.

What he did sounds simple but is very difficult. He made a special liquid from leaves and chemicals and he forced the liquid through tiny holes, the way water is forced out of a

Nylon threads are made from chemicals

showerhead. In fact, Chardonnet did use a special
kind of showerhead called a *spinneret*.

When the thin streams of liquid came out
through the tiny holes of the spinneret they
hardened into long threads that looked like silk.
At first they were called "artificial silk."
Later they got the name "rayon."

Ever since, scientists have been experimenting
with this method and we now have many
different fibers, each made from a different
chemical. Nylon is one of them.

Why do we need all these chemical fibers?
Why can't we just use fibers we find in nature?

The answer is that we still use natural fibers,
but we don't have enough for the population of
the world which keeps growing all the time.

A spinneret

In the United States alone, almost six billion yards of cloth were used for clothes in 1970 and over half of that was made with chemical fibers. We just don't have enough natural fibers for all that cloth.

Another reason for chemical fibers is that we can do things with them that we can't do with natural fibers. We can make the same fiber look like wool or cotton or silk. We can make cloth stronger and easier to clean. And from these chemical fibers we can make clothes that never need to be pressed.

Still, we need the natural fibers, too. No one has yet invented a chemical fiber which feels as nice as cotton or wool. Scientists may do that one day, but they haven't done it yet.

A modern power loom can weave six yards of cloth an hour

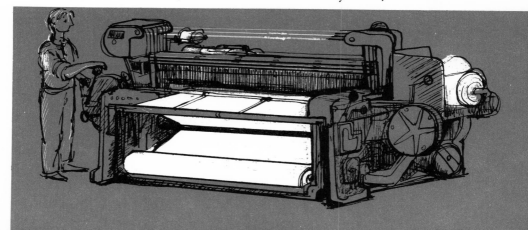

13. So Many Clothes

Six billion yards of cloth make almost six billion pieces of clothing. That's about 25 pieces of clothing every year for each man, woman, and child in the United States.

Of course, that's just arithmetic. Some people have more than that; others have less. People in other countries don't have nearly so many clothes. And people in bygone times certainly didn't have as many.

In earlier times people had one set of clothes for workdays and a special set for Sundays and holidays. They used the workday clothes until they were worn out. Only then did they get new ones. But the Sunday and holiday clothes often lasted a lifetime. They were well made.

Today, most of our clothes are made by machines in factories. There are more than 25,000 factories in the United States making all kinds of clothes and more than a million people work in these factories. This all began about 130 years ago when the sewing machine was invented.

It's very easy for us now to walk into a store and buy a shirt—if we have the money. But in some ways it's a lot more difficult than it was in earlier times when people bought the shirt

An early sewing machine

from the man or woman who made it. Today, a great many things must happen before we can get a shirt. This is the way it goes:

1. First, the cotton fiber must be grown by a farmer; or the chemical fiber must be made in a factory.

2. Then, the fiber must be sent to another factory where it is spun into yarn.

3. Next, the yarn must be taken to a mill where it is woven or knitted into cloth.

4. The cloth is then sent to another factory where it is dyed in many colors or printed with designs. It may also be treated with chemicals so the shirt won't need to be pressed.

5. Next, the cloth is sent to a shirt factory. Here, it must be cut up into many small pieces

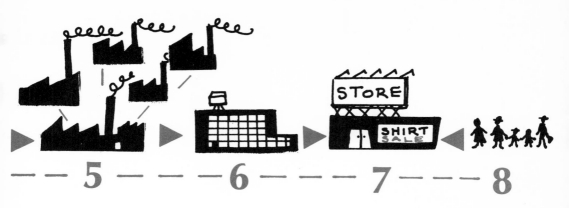

and then sewn together into a shirt. The sewing thread and the buttons have to come from still other factories. And the shirt has to be pressed and put into a box or plastic bag, which comes from a different factory.

6. Then the shirt is stored in a warehouse.

7. From the warehouse it goes to a store.

8. Finally, we go to the store to buy it.

You can see why it takes thousands of people to make it possible for us to buy a shirt.

This is a lot different from the way it was in Greek times when a shirt was simply a big piece of cloth which wasn't cut or sewn, or made in a factory, or sold in a store. In those days most people probably didn't own more than one shirt at a time.

Six billion pieces of clothing! Do we need so many? Of course not! It's nice to have them, but we certainly don't need them all. The only reason we have so many is because we like to dress up. We like to be in fashion. That's the only reason for six billion pieces of clothing.

Some people think we have far too many clothes today. They think it's a great waste for us to throw them away before they're worn out. A lot of young people feel like that. They wear their jeans until they're worn out. Then they patch them to make them last longer, just as people used to do in pioneer days.

14. Clothes of the Future

What will clothes be like 100 years from now? Imagine this:

- Plastic suits with heat and air conditioning.
- Plastic dresses that change color.
- Throwaway clothes that never need to be cleaned and that would dissolve in water without causing pollution.

- Clothes with built-in radio and TV.
- Clothes made without sewing. The parts will be stuck together by electricity.
- Clothes as strong as steel and as soft as cotton. One set of clothes will last forever.

It might come to that if the population of the world keeps on growing, because there might not be enough fiber or cloth to go around.

But that would be boring, wouldn't it? People have always liked to change their clothes, as you can see from reading this book. And they will want to do the same in the future. You can be quite sure of that.

Index

Africa, clothes of, 25
America, clothes of, in Colonial
    times, 30–31, 42;
  of pioneers, 32–33;
  of Indians, 34–36;
  amount of clothing in, 56
aprons, 6, 35, 47
armor, 47

Bloomer, Amelia, 43
blouse, 40
bodice, 5
Boone, Daniel, 36
boots, 7, 44
boys, *see* children
breeches, 31, 42, 48
buttons, 5–7, 10

capes, 41
caps, lace, 31
cedar bark, cloth of, 34
Chardonnet, Hilaire, 53–54
chemicals, fiber from, 53–55
children, clothes for, 4–7, 9, 14, 28,
    38, 42, 43, 46, 56
China, pants in, 42
chitons, 22, 40
climate, and clothes, 12–13, 15, 20,
    23–25, 34
cloth, for clothes, 9–10, 19–22, 32, 34,
    53–55;
  making of, 17–18;
  draping of, 20;
  machine and hand made, 32, 52–
    53;
  description of, 50;
chemicals, fiber from, 53–55
  in 1970, 55, 56;
  see also spinning, weaving, knit-
    ting, looms, *and kinds of cloth*
clothes, of today, 4, 23–25, 36, 37, 41,
    42, 44, 56–59;
  new, 8, 10, 57
handmade, 8, 32;
  reasons for wearing, 12–15, 47;
  first, 15–18;
  of long ago, 19–37, 40–46, 56, 59;
  fitting of, 26–27;
  changes in, 26–33, 37–46;
  machine-made, 57–59;
  need for, 60;
  of future, 61–62
coats, 7, 41
corsets, 46
cotton, clothes of, 5, 7, 25, 53, 55;
  experiment with, 17;
  cloth from, 18, 19, 21, 34;
  artificial, 55
countries, clothes in, 19–28; *see also*
    names of countries
customs, clothes and, 20

decoration, clothes as, 14, 38;
  of bodies, 15
deerskin, clothes of, 34–36
doublets, 41
dresses, 6, 27, 31, 33, 35

England, clothes in, 28, 30
Eskimos, and clothes, 12

factories, 57–59
fashion, 37–46, 60
fibers, 17, 32, 50;
  natural, 18, 53–55;
  chemical, 53–55
flax, 18, 19, 53
France, king of, 39
future, clothes of, 61–62

girls, *see* children
goats, wool of, 16
Gold Rush, 11
Greece, ancient, clothes of, 21–23, 25,
    26, 40, 42, 44, 59